MINIBEASTS UP CLOSE

Wasps
Up Close

Greg Pyers

www.raintreepublishers.co.uk
Visit our website to find out more information about **Raintree** books.

To order:
- ☎ Phone 44 (0) 1865 888112
- 🖹 Send a fax to 44 (0) 1865 314091
- 🖳 Visit the Raintree Bookshop at **www.raintreepublishers.co.uk** to browse our catalogue and order online.

Published in 2005 by Heinemann Library
a division of Harcourt Education Australia,
18–22 Salmon Street, Port Melbourne Victoria 3207 Australia
(a division of Reed International Books Australia Pty Ltd,
ABN 70 001 002 357).
Visit the Heinemann Library website at
www.heinemannlibrary.com.au

First published in Great Britain by Raintree,
Halley Court, Jordan Hill, Oxford OX2 8EJ,
part of Harcourt Education.
Raintree is a registered trademark of Harcourt Education Ltd.

Ⓡ A Reed Elsevier company

© Reed International Books Australia Pty Ltd 2005
First published in paperback in 2006

ISBN 1 74070 234 4 (hardback)
09 08 07 06 05
10 9 8 7 6 5 4 3 2 1

ISBN 1 844 43807 4 (paperback)
10 09 08 07 06
10 9 8 7 6 5 4 3 2 1

Editorial: Anne McKenna, Carmel Heron
Design: Kerri Wilson, Stella Vassiliou
Photo research: Legend Images, Wendy Duncan
Production: Tracey Jarrett
Illustration: Rob Mancini

Typeset in Officina Sans 19/23 pt
Film separations by Print & Publish, Port Melbourne
Printed and bound in China by South China
Printing Company Ltd.

The paper used to print this book comes from sustainable resources.

National Library of Australia Cataloguing-in-Publication data:

Greg, Pyers.
    Wasps up close.

    Includes index.
    For primary students.
    ISBN 1 74070 234 4. (hardback)
    ISBN 1 844 43807 4. (paperback)

    1. Wasps – Juvenile literature. I. Title.
    (Series: Minibeasts up close).

595.79

Acknowledgements
The publisher would like to thank the following for permission to reproduce photographs: Auscape/Kathie Atkinson: p. **4**, /John Cancalosi: p. **7**, /Oxford Scientific Films/Paulo de Oliveira: p. **17**, /Anne & Jacques Six: p. **24**; Australian Picture Library/ Corbis: p. **27**; William M. Ciesla, Forest Health Management International: p. **28**; Denis Crawford – Graphic Science: p. **16**; Lochman Transparencies/Wade Hughes: p. **11**, /Jiri Lochman: pp. **6, 10, 13, 21**; © PREMAPHOTOS/Naturepl. com: p. **20**; photolibrary.com/SPL: pp. **12, 14, 25, 26**; Sergio Piumatti: p. **29**; Robert Shantz: p. **22**; © Paul Zborowski: pp. **5, 8, 15, 23**.

Cover photograph of a European wasp reproduced with the permission of Auscape/Anne & Jacques Six.

Contents

Words that are printed in bold, **like this**, are explained in the glossary on page 31.

Amazing wasps!

Have you ever seen a wasp? Perhaps it was buzzing around you while you were having a picnic. You may have seen a wasp carrying an insect, or even attacking a spider. Maybe you have seen many wasps near an underground nest. When you look at them up close, wasps really are amazing animals.

European wasps are attracted to sweet foods, such as this orange.

There are about 20,000 kinds, or species, of wasps.

What are wasps?

Wasps are insects. They are related to bees and ants. Insects have six legs and no bones inside their bodies. Instead, their bodies have a hard, waterproof skin. This skin is called an **exoskeleton**.

Most wasps have two pairs of wings and females have a sting at the end of their body. Many wasps are brightly coloured.

What 'wasp' means

The word 'wasp' comes from an old word meaning 'weave'. This is because many wasp **species** build paper nests that look as if they have been woven.

Where do wasps live?

Most **species** of wasps live in warm climates. Those that live where winters are cold are active only during the summer. For example, European wasps shelter over the cold months in wood piles and in cracks in trees.

Habitat

A **habitat** is a place where an animal lives. Wasps live in many types of habitats. There are wasps in deserts, rainforests, grasslands, wetlands and along coasts.

The sand wasp lives in dry habitats.

Solitary and social

Most wasp species are **solitary**. This means that they live alone. But some species of wasps live together in large **colonies**.

Nest-builders

Most wasps build nests. Some species build nests from mud. Other species use wood to make paper nests. Many wasp species simply dig holes in the ground or use old spider holes. Some species use the holes made in wood by beetle grubs.

Digging time

The American great golden digger wasp takes between 15 minutes and 4.5 hours to dig a nest, depending on the type of soil.

These wasps have built a nest on a tree trunk.

Wasp body parts

A wasp's body has three main parts. These are the head, the **thorax** and the **abdomen** (<u>ab</u>-da-men). A wasp has a very narrow waist between its thorax and abdomen.

The head

A wasp's head has two eyes, two feelers called **antennae** (an-<u>ten</u>-ay) and mouthparts. There may be stiff hairs on a wasp's head.

wing

head

antenna

eye

thorax

abdomen

leg

The thorax

A wasp's wings and legs are attached to the thorax. The thorax has strong muscles inside it to make the wings and legs work.

Most wasps have four wings and can fly. The females of a few **species** of wasps do not have wings.

The abdomen

The wasp's food is digested inside its abdomen. This means that the food is broken down into tiny pieces.

In females, eggs are produced inside the abdomen. Females have a sting at the end of the abdomen.

Body shape and colour

Many wasp species are brightly coloured. Often they are yellow, red and black. Some species have quite broad bodies, while others are very slender.

Mouthparts and eating

Adult wasps and wasp **larvae** eat quite different food.

Food for adults

Adult wasps feed mainly on **nectar**. Nectar is a sweet **liquid** made by flowers. They also drink tree **sap** that might seep from a broken branch.

Food for larvae

Most wasp larvae are carnivorous, which means that they eat other animals. Wasp larvae cannot hunt their own food. Adult wasps have to do this for them. They hunt for spiders, caterpillars and insects. Wasps use their stings to inject venom into their prey. Venom is a poison that kills the prey or puts it to sleep.

This mud-dauber wasp is drinking from a flower.

Mouthparts

Adult wasps have quite large jaws, called **mandibles**. Mandibles cut **prey** into small pieces. Many wasps eat the prey and carry it to their larvae. There, the wasp vomits food for the larvae to eat.

Wasps have strong mandibles for biting.

mandible

Eyes and seeing

The **sense** of sight is very important to wasps. It helps them to find their **prey**. It also helps them to find their nests and mates. Sight allows wasps to look out for **predators**, such as birds.

Compound eyes

A wasp has two large **compound eyes**. These are eyes that are made up of thousands of very small eyes. Each small eye faces in a slightly different direction. Together, these small eyes give the wasp an excellent view to the front, side and back.

This close-up photo shows how the small eyes of a wasp's compound eye fit tightly together.

compound eye

Ocelli see only
light and dark.

ocelli

More eyes

A wasp also has three very simple eyes on top
of its head. These are called **ocelli** (oh-<u>selly</u>).

Finding home

When a wasp leaves its nest, it
often flies around the entrance
before moving off. It checks to
see what is around the nest, such
as stones or twigs. These will
help the wasp find its nest again.

Special sight

Wasps can see a type of
light called ultraviolet
light. Insect traps in shops
have ultraviolet lights that
attract wasps. When the
wasp enters the trap, it is
killed by an electric shock.

Antennae and sensing

Wasps do not only use their eyes to **sense**.

Knowing who is who

When two wasps meet, they check each other out with their **antennae** to find out whether they come from the same nest. Wasps from the same nest carry the same smells. Male and female wasps recognize each other by the smells they give off.

These European wasps are checking each other out with their antennae.

Smell

A wasp can wave its antennae about to pick up food smells. When the wasp reaches the food, it uses its antennae to taste it.

Touch

Antennae are important for feeling things. For example, when a wasp builds a nest, the antennae help to measure the size of each **cell** the eggs will be laid in.

This European wasp is sensing its food with its antennae.

Wings and flying

Most **species** of wasps are strong fliers. But there are some wasps that have no wings.

Four wings

Most wasps have four wings. Each back wing is attached to a front wing by a row of hooks.

This is a close-up photo of a wasp's wing.

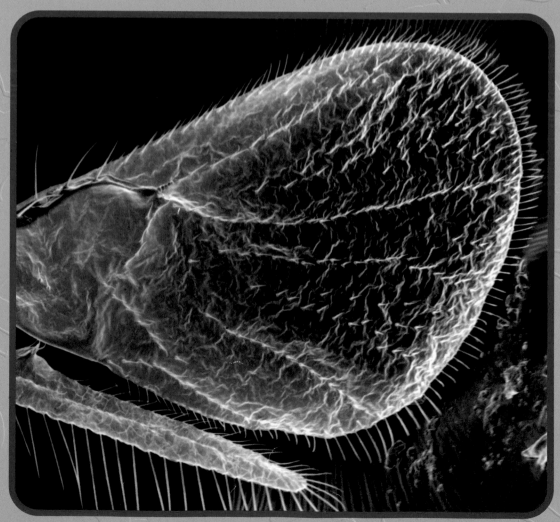

Fast beating

The buzzing sound you hear when a wasp is close by is made by the fast beating of its wings.

Making the wings move

A wasp's wings are attached to the **thorax**. There are strong muscles inside the thorax that move the top of the thorax in and out. As the thorax moves, the wings move with it.

A wasp's wings beat up and down around 200 times a second.

Wingless wasps

The females of a hairy wasp called the velvet ant do not have wings. These wasps lay their eggs in the nests of other wasps and bees.

Inside a wasp

Wasps have blood that is bluish and clear, and a heart that is a tube.

Blood

A wasp's blood moves through the spaces in its body. The blood travels from the head, through the **thorax** and into the **abdomen**. From there, the heart pumps it forward again.

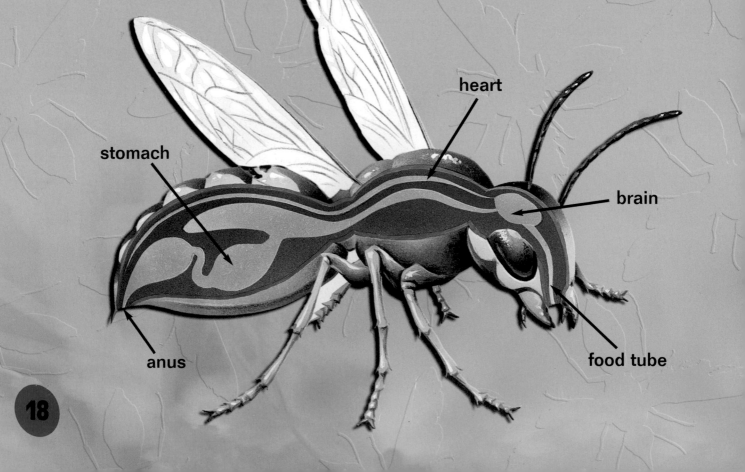

heart

stomach

brain

anus

food tube

How do wasps get air?

A wasp does not breathe through its mouth. Air gets into its body through tiny holes called **spiracles** (<u>spi</u>-ra-kels). There is a row of spiracles down each side of the wasp's body.

What happens to food?

The wasp's **liquid** food passes from the mouth, down a tube to the stomach. As the food moves, it is broken down to release **nutrients**. A wasp needs nutrients to stay alive. Waste passes out through the anus.

The brain

A wasp's brain gets information that it **senses** through its **antennae** and eyes. It sends messages to the rest of the body about what to do.

Wasp nests

Many wasps build nests. The nests are where the wasp **larvae** grow.

Burrows and mud nests

Many **solitary** wasps build their nests in burrows. The wasps dig the burrows themselves or use the old burrows of beetles or spiders. Some wasps, such as the potter wasp, build mud nests. These are vase-shaped and hang from trees or rock ledges. The mud-dauber wasp builds long tubes of mud that hang together under bridges and roofs.

This wasp is building the entrance to its mud nest.

Paper nests

Wasps that live in groups called **colonies** build large nests. They bite off bits of plants or old wood and chew these with **saliva**. The mixture is spread out in very thin layers and dries into paper. It is then shaped into **cells** where the queen will lay her eggs. She will lay just one egg in each cell.

Some paper nests are attached to a branch. Others are underground, in cupboards or even in the wall spaces of houses.

This wasp nest is made from paper.

Wasp colonies

European wasps may live in colonies. There may be more than 100,000 wasps in a colony.

Solitary wasps' life cycle

Solitary wasps live alone, except when males and females come together to **mate**.

Hunting

After mating, a female solitary wasp hunts. The **prey** is not for her, but for her young. Different **species** of solitary wasps hunt for different prey. The world's largest wasp, the tarantula hawk, hunts for spiders. When she finds her prey, she injects it with **venom** to paralyse it. This means that the prey cannot move.

This tarantula hawk wasp is attacking a spider. Tarantula hawk wasps can be up to five centimetres long.

Laying eggs

The wasp then takes her catch to her nest. She may have to drag it if it is too heavy to fly with. She lays one or more eggs on the prey. She then pushes the prey into the nest and seals the entrance.

When an egg hatches, the **larva** feeds on the prey. When the larva stops growing, it wraps itself in a case called a **cocoon**. In a few weeks, an adult wasp emerges from the cocoon.

A wasp that eats other wasps

The cuckoo wasp lays its eggs in the nests of hunter wasps. When the larvae hatch out, they eat the hunter wasp larvae.

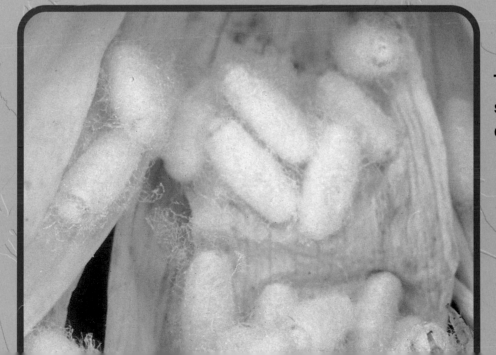

These are solitary wasp cocoons.

A European wasp colony

European wasps commonly live in groups called **colonies**.

Laying eggs

In spring, a single European wasp wakes from her winter's sleep. This wasp is a queen and she will begin a new colony. In three days, she builds a nest with about nine paper **cells**. She lays an egg in each cell.

European wasps are also found in North America and Australia.

Each wasp larva stays in its own cell until it becomes an adult.

Larvae hatch

About six days after laying, a **larva** hatches from each egg. Now, as well as continuing to build her nest, the queen must go hunting. She uses her sting to kill insects and her jaws to break them into small pieces. She carries the insects back to the nest to feed her larvae.

Wasp glue

Wasp larvae glue themselves inside their cells so that they cannot fall out.

The larvae grow quickly. After 15 days, each larva completely fills its own cell. It stops eating and builds a silk **cocoon** around itself. It is now called a **pupa**.

Worker wasps

In two weeks, the **pupa** becomes an adult wasp.
It tears open its **cocoon** and crawls from its **cell**.
This wasp is a worker.

The life of a worker wasp

At first, workers stay inside the nest. They clean
cells, feed **larvae** and make repairs. After a few
days, workers leave the nest. They collect wood
to make paper for expanding the nest. When they
are older, workers hunt for insects and
bring them back to the nest.
They also collect **nectar**.
After two, three or four
weeks, a worker's
life is over.

This new adult wasp
is crawling from its cell,
ready to begin work.

Queens and males

Queen wasps grow from larvae that are fed twice as much as other larvae. In late summer, male wasps and queens leave the nest. The queens **mate** with the males. The males die and the queens look for shelter for their winter sleep. In spring, each queen will begin a new **colony**.

The colony dies

By winter, all the workers in the European wasp colony will have died of cold and hunger. The nest will be abandoned.

This queen European wasp is drinking nectar.

27

Wasps and us

Most wasps do not affect people. Some wasp **species** are very helpful to people, and others are pests.

Wasp pests and helpers

The female sirex wasp lays her eggs in pine wood. When she lays, she also adds a **fungus** to the wood. This fungus makes the wood soft, and easy for the **larvae** to chew. The fungus can also kill the pine tree. Another type of wasp has been used to control sirex wasps. They lay their eggs near the sirex eggs. When they hatch, the wasp larvae eat the sirex eggs and larvae.

Sirex wasp larvae damaged this tree by making tunnels in it as they ate.

Stings

An open can of soft drink outdoors can attract a wasp inside for a sweet drink. If someone drinks from that can, the wasp may sting. This can cause swelling inside the mouth. This can be so bad that the person finds it hard to breathe and needs medical help.

Important wasps

Wasps are very important to farmers. As a wasp drinks **nectar** from flowers, **pollen** is carried from flower to flower. Pollen is a yellow powder that makes fruit and seeds grow. Wasps also kill many insect pests.

Sweet drinks attract wasps, so people should take care when drinking outdoors.

Find out for yourself

You may hear a wasp before you see it. The sound of their wings can be quite loud. Watch what the wasp is doing. Be careful not to disturb it. Wasps can attack people and their sting is very painful.

Books to read

Living Nature: Insects, Angela Royston (Chrysalis Children's Books, 2003)

Looking at Minibeasts: Ants, Bees and Wasps, Sally Morgan (Belitha Press, 2001)

Using the Internet

Explore the Internet to find out more about wasps. Websites can change, so do not worry if the links below no longer work. Use a search engine, such as www.yahooligans.com or www.internet4kids.com, and type in a keyword such as 'wasp', or the name of a particular wasp **species**.

Websites

http://ohioline.osu.edu/hyg-fact/2000/2078.html
This site has interesting information about mud-dauber wasps.

http://ohioline.osu.edu/hyg-fact/2000/2077.html
Read about paper wasps and hornets at this site.

Glossary

abdomen   last of the three main sections of an insect

antenna   (plural: antennae) feeler on an insect's head

cell   small container, like a small room

cocoon   bag in which a wasp larva becomes an adult wasp

colony   (plural: colonies) large numbers of wasps living together in a nest

compound eye   eye made up of many parts

exoskeleton   hard outside skin of an insect

fungus   plant-like living thing that feeds on plants and animals

habitat   place where an animal lives

larva   (plural: larvae) grub stage in a wasp's life between the egg and the adult wasp

liquid   something that is runny, not hard, such as juice

mandible   jaw

mate   when a male and a female come together to produce young

nectar   sweet liquid inside flowers

nutrients   parts of food that are important for an animal's health

ocelli   small eyes on a wasp's head that sense light

pollen   substance on flowers made of dry, dusty grains, usually yellow

predator   animal that kills and eats other animals

prey   animal that is caught and eaten by other animals

pupa   (plural: pupae) stage of an insect's life when it changes from a larva to an adult

saliva   liquid from the mouth

sap   juice inside a plant

sense   how an animal knows what is going on around it, such as seeing, hearing or smelling

solitary   living by itself

species   type or kind of animal

spiracle   tiny air hole

thorax   chest part of an insect

vibration   fast shaking movement

Index